The Long Trail Home

John Manos, Loretta West,
and Natalie West
Illustrated by Diana Kizlauskas

Rigby®

Level T Guided Reading Chapter Book

On Our Way to English: *The Long Trail Home*

© 2004 by Rigby
1000 Hart Road
Barrington, IL 60010
www.rigby.com

Text by John Manos, Loretta West, and Natalie West
Illustrated by Diana Kizlauskas

09 08 07 06 05 04
10 9 8 7 6 5 4 3

Printed in China

ISBN 0-7578-4539-8

Contents

1

"Where Am I?"

Before she even opened her eyes, Paula knew that she was in a strange place. She wasn't lying on the lumpy straw mattress she'd had since she was a small child, and the room didn't have the familiar smell of the wood stove that had burned in the corner of her family's kitchen. She heard a woman's soft voice that was not her mother's. Something was terribly wrong. "Where am I?" she thought.

Then it all started coming back to her—she remembered *Mamá* and *Papá* becoming ill with the yellow fever that had swept through Texas in the early spring of 1873, and she remembered giving *Mamá* and *Papá* water and broth as they lay in bed, so sick that they could hardly talk.

Paula also remembered the morning when she had become ill. She had tried to keep caring for her parents, but the fever that had overcome her made Paula feel sicker than she ever had in her 11 years. She felt as though her body was on fire!

The last thing she remembered was finally stumbling out of their small house, so sick that she could barely walk, to look for someone who could help them.

When Paula's eyes opened at last, she saw her grandfather, Benito Aguilar, sitting in a wooden chair beside her bed, and behind him a woman who must have been nursing Paula through her fever. Paula realized that she must be in the mission hospital in San Antonio, but how did she get here?

6

Their house was in a settlement 20 miles away from San Antonio. When Benito saw Paula's eyes open, he smiled sadly, and she knew without being told that *Mamá* and *Papá* were dead.

"*Mamá? Papá?*" she began, her voice very weak, but Benito looked down at the floor and then back into her eyes.

"I'm sorry, little one," he said in Spanish, "we have only one another now."

Instantly, Paula knew that everything had changed—sadly, her parents were gone, and nothing would ever be the same again.

Benito drove a chuck wagon (a wagon that held the items they would need for cooking) on the Chisholm Trail, helping to drive cattle from Texas all the way north to the railroad stockyards at Abilene, Kansas. He had no permanent home, just a camp about 80 miles north of Paula's home—or rather, what she used to call home. Paula suddenly realized that she would never again help her mother tend their small garden or help her father gather wood for their cooking stove.

Paula bit her lip and struggled not to cry, reminding herself that she was fortunate, because she had her grandfather, while so many other victims of the fever now had no one.

Paula tried to smile bravely as she reached out to take Benito's hand. "*Sí, Abuelito,*" she replied in Spanish, "we will take care of each other now. At least we have one another."

2

A Girl Named Paul

Nearly a month had passed since Paula left the mission hospital, and she was slowly getting back her strength. Now that Paula was almost healthy again, Benito and his friend McCabe could begin preparing for the next cattle drive. McCabe, a tall man about the same age as Paula's grandfather, was the trail boss for the cattle drive. He arranged with different ranches in Texas to take their cattle north and sell them, and he also hired the young men and teenage boys to drive the cattle.

It was Benito's job to take the chuck wagon ahead of the herd each day, looking for water for the cattle and a good place to spend each night. Benito set up the nightly camps, cooked the food, and served as a kind of doctor for the cattle and the horses, as well as the men in the crew. Benito and McCabe had worked together for many years.

Paula couldn't bear to be separated from her grandfather, so she begged to be allowed to go with him, but there was an unwritten rule that girls and women were forbidden on cattle drives. So McCabe and Benito decided that for as long as the drive took, at no time would the cowboys think there was an 11-year-old girl riding the chuck wagon with Benito, but rather his grandson "Paul" would be along for the drive.

For two weeks, while McCabe hired the cowboys (known as *waddies*), made arrangements to pick up herds of cattle all across north Texas, and assembled enough horses for the long trip, Benito filled the chuck wagon with hundreds of pounds of food—flour, sugar, salt, cornmeal, dried beans, and other things he needed. During this time, the two men tried to teach Paula how to act like a boy.

She put on a pair of pants for the first time in her life, and she put on a wide-brimmed hat that was nothing like anything she had worn in the garden at home. She tried to walk like a boy, by learning to tuck her hands in her belt and chew on a stem of grass. But the most difficult part, Paula decided, was remembering to answer when McCabe or Benito called her "Paul."

Slowly Paula began to look and act like a boy—even though she still wasn't crazy about wearing pants instead of a dress.

"How do boys walk around in anything this tight?" she laughed one day, slapping the legs of her pants.

McCabe winked at her and answered, "I'd probably have even more trouble if I tried to put on a dress."

But now came the worst part of all.

"Why do we have to cut off my hair?" Paula groaned. "Why can't I just tuck it into my hat?"

Her grandfather smiled and shook his head, explaining patiently, "Paula, we will be on the drive for three months or more, and there's no way you could keep your hair hidden under your hat that long."

Paula knew he was right, but it didn't make her feel any better. She could cope with walking, talking, and acting like a boy, but she certainly didn't want to have hair like a boy. Paula's mother used to spend hours brushing and braiding Paula's long, black hair, and the memory of her mother telling her how beautiful her hair was made Paula sad. She tried to push the sadness away, closed her eyes, and muttered, "I'll still be me whether I have long hair or short. Go ahead and get it over with."

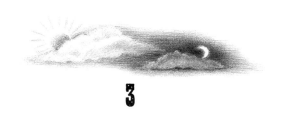

3

The Cattle Drive Begins

Like everyone else in Texas, Paula had heard about the big cattle drives that started a few years after the Civil War ended, but now that she was actually on a cattle drive, she realized that she really knew very little about it. Paula had imagined that the herd moved in one big, solid group, but instead it was more like a long, long line of steers, usually only four or five animals walking side by side with waddies in front, on both sides, and behind the herd. The youngest waddies had the "drags," meaning they were behind the herd, making sure no steers strayed away from the herd. It was an important job, but Paula felt sorry for these boys who spent most days in a cloud of dust.

Most of all, though, Paula couldn't believe how *slow* the trip was! She could have walked north faster than the cattle were moving. Benito explained, "We want these cattle to move slowly and eat their way north because a perfect cattle drive ends with the steers heavier in Kansas than they were in Texas."

As slow as the drive was, Paula wasn't bored. For her, the trip was an adventure, and as they moved into the plains north of San Antonio, the rolling green land seemed magically beautiful as it stretched away to the horizon. She felt as if she could see forever! She loved to see clouds in the distance—even the giant thunderheads with lightning dancing beneath them.

Also, Paula kept busy helping Benito on the chuck wagon every day as they moved ahead of the herd. When they were five or six miles up the trail, they stopped to prepare a noon meal for the crew. Meals took a long time because

the waddies ate in shifts so that half of them
were always tending the herd. Then after all of
the workers had eaten, and she had cleaned the
plates, knives, and forks and stored them in the
big box at the back of the chuck wagon, she
and Benito set out again in search of a good
place to spend the night. McCabe told her he
wouldn't trust anyone other than Benito with
this job—Benito always found the best spots
for a nighttime campsite.

Along the trail northward, they stopped several times to collect more cattle, until the herd had more than 1,500 steers in it and the line of cattle during the day was more than half a mile long!

Though Paula found life on the trail exciting, she realized that the biggest problem with the long, lazy days was that she had too much time to think about *Mamá* and *Papá* and the home she would never know again.

4

Comanches

"Riders are coming," Paula shouted as she ran down a small hill to the chuck wagon, "three of them!"

Benito looked up from the harness he was cleaning, his eyes narrowing as he saw the fear in Paula's face. Visitors were not usually welcomed on cattle drives. Out in the wide-open spaces of the Texas plains, the arrival of any stranger could mean danger. Too often visitors turned out to be thieves looking to steal cattle.

Benito walked up the hill and stared into the distance, where he saw that indeed, three riders were approaching, all with long, dark hair in braids that fell past their shoulders. They were riding ponies, and they had several more ponies with them. He didn't think they looked like rustlers, but he did think they looked like Comanches.

Paula clutched at his hand, remembering terrible stories she had heard about conflicts between the Comanches and the settlers in western Texas. "Do you think they're dangerous?" she asked, her voice weak.

Benito watched the riders for a few seconds longer, and then he shook his head, saying "I don't think so, but you never know. Just stay calm, and we'll see what they want."

A short time later, the riders approached their camp, and although none of the three men smiled, they held their hands up in greeting. Benito raised his in return and greeted the men in English, but none responded, so he tried Spanish, but still, the stern faces of the men remained like stone masks. Paula tried to be calm, but she began to feel very frightened as the three men studied her closely.

Finally one of the men slid down from his pony and said something, but not surprisingly, Paula didn't understand his language. Then he began to move his hands, making signs to show what he wanted, and Paula was amazed—now she thought she did understand him!

"*Abuelito,*" Paula cried, "I think he wants to trade his ponies for some steers!" She picked up a stick and began to make simple drawings in the dirt, beginning with a steer with long horns.

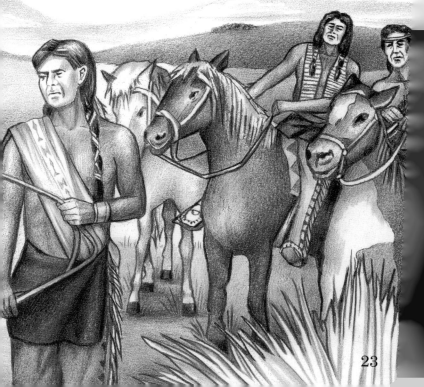

For the first time, the Comanche man smiled. He spoke again and nodded, pointing at her drawing and his ponies, and then he opened his hands as if he was describing a large crowd and pointed at his mouth and stomach, then the drawing of the steer. "They're hungry, *Abuelito*," Paula said, "and they want to trade their ponies for food to take to their people!"

The man reached for the stick and drew four more steers next to Paula's drawing. He then pointed at the three extra ponies the men had with them, and he walked to the ponies and pulled them by their reins so that Benito and Paula could see them. Paula reached out to touch one of the ponies, a pretty mare that was white all over, except for one large brown spot on her left shoulder. The Comanche man smiled when he saw that Paula liked the pony, and he offered her its reins. Several times he said *Nah-ee-vee*. The others grinned at him and repeated the word.

Just then, McCabe, who was about a mile ahead of the herd, rode up. Benito explained what the men wanted and then said, "I think the white pony would make a good horse for Paul, don't you?" McCabe smiled and nodded his head in agreement.

As the three Comanche men rode away toward the setting sun, herding along the five steers they had traded for the ponies, Paula said, "I'm going to call her Nobby—it sounds like *Nah-ee-vee*. I wonder what *Nah-ee-vee* means." When she hugged the pony's neck, she knew that she and Nobby would be friends for a long time.

5

Stampede!

Every day Paula rode Nobby as much as she could. She talked to the pony, brushed her coat and mane each evening, and brought her treats, like apples and carrots. By the time Nobby had been with Paula for only two weeks, the pony would trot out of the small herd of extra horses to greet her.

Paula enjoyed riding Nobby so much that she offered to join the waddies on the trail. Each night the head rider would stop the lead steers near the camp that Benito had made around the chuck wagon, but far enough away so that dust didn't get into their food. Then the other cowboys would lead the rest of the cattle into a large, tighter group to bed down. As night fell, pairs of waddies took turns watching over the herd, riding slowly in opposite directions around the cattle. Finally Paula was allowed to ride along on one of these watches.

Paula enjoyed these night rides. A beautiful calm had settled on the plains, and the dark blue sky was filled with twinkling stars.

At night the steers were easily startled, so all the time the waddies were on watch, they sang, whistled, or talked to themselves to let the steers know they were there. The sounds of coyotes, wolves, or panthers in the distance would make the steers jumpy and restless, so the cowboys watched to make sure the wild animals didn't get too close. The cowboys protected the herd as best they could. But there was one thing that cowboys couldn't do anything about—a thunderstorm!

One night while Paula was riding along with the cowboys on the first watch, a storm began. Even before the rain started to fall, a loud thunderclap had startled the steers, and many had jumped to their feet. In a flash of lightning, Paula saw McCabe riding toward her. He was calm but concerned about her.

"I'd like you to go back to the wagon," he said, "because if this herd gets scared and starts running, things could get pretty nasty. Stampedes can be mighty dangerous—especially for a young girl—I mean boy, like you."

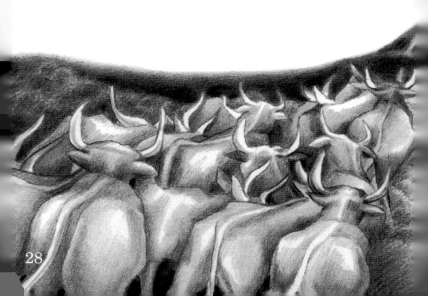

Just as Paula was turning Nobby to leave, another loud crash of thunder echoed overhead, causing the steers that were still lying down to jump to their feet. Those that were already standing suddenly started running straight toward Paula and McCabe!

"Ride!" McCabe shouted. Nobby seemed to understand the danger as well as Paula did, and the pony turned and galloped ahead of the steers while Paula held on for dear life. She could hear thousands of hooves rumbling

behind her, and she turned in the saddle to see the cattle running hard through the pounding rain. Paula tried to guide Nobby out of the way of the cattle, but just as she thought she had reached a safe spot, a silvery bolt of lightning slashed through the sky, followed by a boom of thunder so loud that Paula thought she might go deaf. Nobby reared and Paula fell off the pony.

Terrified, Paula rolled on the ground, but fortunately, the steers charged past her, kicking mud into the air. Nobby stood nearby, but Paula couldn't get hold of the pony's reins.

McCabe galloped up and grabbed Nobby's reins, calling out to Paula, "Are you all right?"

"I'm fine," Paula answered, and when McCabe rode off after the cattle, Paula got on Nobby and followed. Finally the panicking steers became tired, slowed to a trot, and then stopped.

Paula rode up to McCabe and asked, "What do we do now?"

"We'll hold these steers here for now," he answered, "and pull the herd together in the morning." He looked down at her. "You stayed clear-headed, Paula—I mean Paul. You did well."

Paula grinned while patting Nobby's neck. They had survived a stampede!

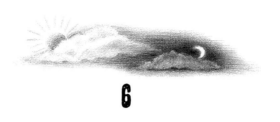

6

To the Rescue

It was dusk, a few days after the big stampede, and the men were just riding in for the night as Benito finished cooking a big pot of stew. Paula was just about to put a pan of biscuits on the rack above the fire when they heard one of the cowboys shouting as he rode toward the camp.

"Mr. McCabe," he yelled as he neared, "around 200 head strayed from the herd about a mile back, and we need some help rounding them up."

McCabe looked at the sky and realized that they had little daylight left, so he started barking orders, telling two waddies to stay with the main herd and sending everyone else back to collect the missing cattle. Benito moved the stew pot away from the fire, covered it, and walked off to saddle a horse. Paula decided to saddle Nobby so that they could help, too.

Paula and Nobby were just a short distance from camp when Paula heard a noise coming from a nearby ditch. "Maybe a steer is trapped," she thought. Paula touched Nobby lightly with her heels to get the pony moving and headed into the ditch, but then the pony stopped suddenly, her nostrils flaring, her eyes wide with fear. In the gathering darkness, Paula could see the young steer, hardly more than a calf, crying out and spinning around, swinging his small horns from side to side as three snarling coyotes circled!

Paula shouted for help, but no response came. She knew there wasn't much time, so without another thought, Paula sent Nobby into motion, charging into the ditch and straight at the coyotes. She screamed at them and swung her coiled rope, trying to scare the animals away. One coyote snapped at the pony,

and Nobby reared onto her hind legs, whinnying with fear. Paula clung to the reins and tried to hold tight with her knees but once again fell from the saddle as Nobby dashed from the ditch.

Paula leaped to her feet, so furious that she wasn't even afraid, knowing that it was up to her to save the steer. She kept lashing at the growling coyotes with her rope. She charged

35

one coyote, and just as her knotted rope slapped its snout, Bret and Joaquín, two young waddies, came galloping up, scaring the coyotes back into the darkness.

As the cowboys rode into the ditch, they were grinning in awe. "Did you see that?" asked Joaquín.

"I couldn't believe my eyes!" replied Bret as he put his rope around the steer's neck while Joaquín rode out to catch Nobby.

Later around the campfire, Joaquín and Bret told the story over and over again, telling how Paul bravely stood his ground and fought off three coyotes with only a rope, all to save one steer.

"I'll tell you," one of the young men said, "we have with us the bravest 11-year-old boy in all of Texas! Three cheers for Paul!"

As the men all cheered, even Paula's grandfather looked at her differently, smiling with pride. At first Paula had felt proud of herself, too, but when she thought about the coyotes, her knees started to shake. For the first time, she realized how dangerous it had been to take on three coyotes by herself. Suddenly Paula was very tired, and all she really wanted to do was curl up in a blanket and go to sleep.

7

A Close Call

In the morning, Paula realized that she had torn her coat during her fight with the coyotes, so she wrapped a blanket around her shoulders and threaded a needle to repair her sleeve. It was a lovely, bright, cool morning, and the cattle were already moving their slow way along the trail, munching grass as they walked.

Paula sat on a bedroll next to the chuck wagon and got to work, even though she realized that the torn sleeve didn't make that much difference. Almost every waddy had a torn shirt and patched pants, but Paula couldn't stand to have holes in her clothes.

"*Mamá* would be proud of these stitches," she thought, as she neatly sewed up the tear. As she finished and broke the end of the thread with her teeth, Paula became aware that Bret and two other cowboys were staring at her strangely as they ate cold biscuits, and not one of them was talking.

"Where did you ever learn to sew like that?" Bret asked at last.

"*Mamá* taught me," Paula answered, proudly holding up her expertly mended coat, as if it was the most natural thing in the world. But then she realized her mistake. While some men on a cattle drive might have learned to sew out of necessity, there wasn't much of a chance that there would be even one boy in all of Texas who knew how to make fine, delicate stitches like those Paula had used to repair her coat.

"I'll tell you, Paul," Bret said with his mouth full of biscuit, "you are one uncommon fellow. First you're willing to fight three hungry coyotes barehanded, and then it turns out that you can sew better than my sister!"

Paula decided to change the subject quickly. "Well, I'd better help clean up," she said as she pulled her hat lower to cover her blushing cheeks.

Just then Benito stepped around from the back of the chuck wagon and said, "Don't you boys think you ought to let the night shift come in for breakfast?" As the waddies left to mount their horses, Benito glanced over at Paula with a look that seemed to say, "Be more careful." Somehow the morning didn't seem as pretty as it had just a few minutes earlier.

8

Texas Fever

The stockyards in Abilene, Kansas, would be the last stop on the long trail north, but the cattle drive's final stop in Texas would be the Double-A Ranch, near Red River Station. McCabe had contracted with the Double-A to drive 400 head of cattle to Abilene, so he rode up to the house expecting to meet with Arthur Andrews, the ranch's owner, whose initials gave the ranch its name. Instead, he was met with bad news: Arthur Andrews had died, leaving the ranch in the hands of his widow, Maggie. Maggie told McCabe that she wouldn't be able to send her cattle to Abilene. Her foreman, the man who used to run the ranch, had quit his job and left the ranch just four days earlier. He had told her that the herd was infected with "Texas fever," a cattle disease that caused northern states to stop Texas cattle from crossing their borders. Maggie had put the sick steers in a separate corral from the healthy steers.

McCabe was afraid that the herd he was driving might become infected, too. But Benito said, "Before we leave, I'd like to see those sick steers."

Maggie led them to the small corral near one of the barns behind the ranch house. Benito studied the animals in the corral, watching them and touching them, and looking in their eyes and their mouths. Then he put his head against their sides to listen to their hearts. Finally he stepped away, frowning their hearts. Finally he stepped away, frowning and shaking his head, and said, "Mrs. Andrews, I don't think these cattle have Texas fever. I don't mean to insult the foreman you used to have, but I think he's wrong about your cattle. I think maybe they just ate some bad weeds and got sick."

"How can I know for sure?" Maggie asked. "If anyone thinks my cattle have Texas fever, they won't buy them, and more important, my reputation for raising fine cattle will be ruined."

"I'm almost positive that I'm right, but the only way to tell for sure is to wait a week or so," Benito answered.

"Can you stay?" Maggie asked McCabe. "I need you to take my herd to Abilene, and I'll pay the cowboys' wages for the entire week."

McCabe agreed, saying he thought everyone could use a few days' rest, anyway.

As the adults talked, Paula, who was standing behind Benito, realized that

Maggie was staring at her. Paula strutted over to her, trying to walk like a boy, tipped her hat, and said, "Hello, Mrs. Andrews."

"Call me Maggie," the older woman said, a very small smile touching the corners of her mouth. She shook Paula's hand, glanced around, and leaned in close. "How long has it been since you had a real bath, dear, and wouldn't you rather be wearing a dress than that cowboy outfit?"

Benito overheard what Maggie said to Paula, and he gasped, "How could you tell? Everyone else was fooled!"

"Only a bunch of waddies on a long cattle trail would miss it. I took one look at her, and I thought that Paul was really a girl. Then I shook her hand and I knew for sure because only girls have such smooth skin." Maggie laughed, turned to Paula, and said, "Why don't you come inside with me and turn back into a girl for a little while?"

45

9

A Girl Named Paula

One morning as Maggie and Paula were feeding the horses, Maggie asked Paula how Nobby got her name.

Paula explained that the Comanches who had traded the pony for steers kept saying something that sounded like *Nah-ee-vee,* so she made her pony's name sound like the word they were using. To her surprise, Maggie began to laugh.

"I think they may have seen through your disguise," Maggie finally said, "because what they were saying is a Comanche word that means good-looking girl."

Paula blushed and tried to hide her embarrassment. "Well, then the name fits because Nobby is a very good-looking girl."

They had been at the Double-A for a week, and Paula had been spending much of her time with Maggie. She liked Maggie a lot. Being around Maggie made Paula realize how hard it was not having a mother. It did feel good to stop pretending to be a boy even though Paula still wore her pants and boots. Plus, it was nice to sleep in a cozy bed instead of on the cold, hard floor of the chuck wagon.

The week had flown by, and Benito was correct—Maggie's cattle didn't have Texas fever. Paula was sad that they would soon be leaving the ranch to get back on the cattle trail, because the Double-A was the closest thing to a home that Paula had experienced in quite a while. She knew that her home was now on the trail with her grandfather, but still, it was nice to imagine what life would be like for her and her grandfather if they could make the Double-A their home. That's why Paula was so shocked when Maggie spoke.

"I can't believe that you men plan to take this girl to Abilene," she said to Benito and McCabe on the last afternoon. "That's a wild, rough town, and it's no place for Paula to be!"

McCabe and Benito agreed, but they shrugged their shoulders, asking, "What else can we do?"

"You can leave Paula here with me," Maggie declared. "She's a smart, brave girl, and she's wonderful company. I'd love to have her here while you finish the trip to Abilene, and then you can pick her up on your way back south."

"But I cannot leave my *Abuelito*," Paula said, her lip trembling. Though secretly wanting to stay, Paula felt guilty about even thinking of leaving her grandfather—he was the only family she had left.

"I hope you will change your mind," Maggie answered, her voice softening. "The same fever that took your parents also killed my husband, my son, and my daughter. My daughter was about your age, and you can't imagine how much I miss having a family." She looked down at Paula, her eyes shining with tears.

As she looked back at Maggie, Paula began to cry, too. Never had she cried so hard in her whole life. She cried for everything she had

lost, for the places she missed, for Maggie's husband and children, and most of all for *Mamá* and *Papá*. She couldn't stop, so Maggie wrapped her arms around Paula's thin shoulders, softly stroked Paula's hair, and kissed the top of her head.

"Maybe," Maggie whispered into the girl's ear, "just maybe, Paula, together we can help one another feel less sad." Paula cried even harder, and Maggie just held her more tightly.

10

The Trail's End

Paula burst out laughing when she saw the waddies' mouths drop open as she walked into the camp at Maggie's side the next morning. Paula was wearing a beautiful dress that had once belonged to Maggie's daughter. She saw Bret's face turn red as Maggie thanked the crew and handed McCabe a pay packet for the extra week. Though Paula's secret had been revealed earlier in the week, this was the first time the cowboys had seen her in a dress, and suddenly they were all very shy.

"I guess this explains the sewing," Bret muttered, shaking his head.

Maggie reached out to shake Benito's hand and said, "Mr. Aguilar, thank you for proving that my herd was healthy, and I want to tell you that I think you're a great cattleman."

"He's the best I've ever known," McCabe said.

"Even more," Maggie continued, "I want to thank you for bringing Paula to me, and I'd like you to think about an idea I had this morning. I need a foreman on this ranch, and Paula needs a home, so here's what I suggest. When you return from Abilene, how would you like to take the job of foreman here on the Double-A?"

Benito smiled, scratched his chin, and looked at McCabe, who grinned back and shrugged.

Maggie said, "You can wait until you get back from Abilene to tell me what you've decided. As for right now, Paula, let's ride around the ranch a little so we can keep out of the way of these fellows."

Paula hugged her grandfather goodbye, but she wasn't sad, because she knew he would be back in just a month or so, perhaps for good. She waved to McCabe and the cowboys as they headed the herd north, and then she got into Maggie's carriage.

Maggie drove the carriage up to the top of a small hill. From there they could see a tree-lined stream winding down from the hills at the north end of the large ranch. In the distance, Paula could see the ranch house surrounded by trees, and in the pasture behind the house she saw her dear Nobby, and beyond the pasture the plains rolled like waves going on forever.

"It's beautiful," Paula said.

"I hope you like it here," said Maggie, smiling as she looked at the wonderful view.

"I love it here," Paula exclaimed, "and I'm so happy you want *Abuelito* to be your foreman!"

Maggie smiled even wider. "I've met many cattlemen, and your grandfather is the best I've ever met," she said. "Even McCabe, who's very good himself, agrees. Learn everything you can from your grandfather, Paula, because I hope that someday the Double-A name is going to stand for Andrews and Aguilar."

For the first time since waking up in the mission hospital, Paula was truly happy. She could almost feel the sadness melting away from her heart. The long trail had led her and her grandfather to Maggie and a new home.